HOW SUFFERING SHOWS GOD'S LOVE

A Paradox Explained

HOW SUFFERING SHOWS GOD'S LOVE

A Paradox Explained

Sonya Contreras

Bull Head Press

Published by Bull Head Press
Squaw Valley, California
Paperback ISBN: 978-0-9990009-3-9
eBook ISBN: 978-0-9990009-4-6

Library of Congress Control Number: 2017915494

Cover Design by Wendy_graphics from Fiverr
Formatting by Joseph Contreras, Jr.
Edited by Titania Porter
Verse editing by Hannah Porter
Typeface: Felix Titling, and Constantia

Printed in the United States of America.

Dear Reader,

Pain opens the heart to search for meaning. We ask God, "Why?" And find He is silent. We question His goodness, love and sovereignty. These questions bring us to Him.

By coming to Him, we learn the deeper answers. We find the love we crave. We discover the God Who wants us to know Him.

This collection of articles leads us to find that meaning, learn those answers and see our God.

If you require more explanations before you approach Him with open arms, read the two books I used: Paul Brand and Philip Yancey in In His Image *provides a heart view of God and C.S. Lewis in* The Problem of Pain *gives the mind's view of God. Or better yet, search the Psalms where you see David's heart poured out before his God and see the answers He finds.*

God is waiting for you to come to Him. He uses pain to get your attention.

May these answers bring you to the Savior where His perfect love is found.

Sonya Contreras

TABLE OF CONTENTS

CAN A GOOD GOD GIVE SUFFERING?

H ave you ever asked, "How can God allow suffering, if God is good?"

There's no easy answer. God is God. If we could understand Him, we would be like God, knowing and able to do everything. We are not, so we will never fully understand.

But, I know that God is good. And He is in control.

If God is good, then what He does is good. He is also in control of everything, even suffering.

People see suffering, and doubt God's goodness or His control.

Can a loving God give pain? Is that good?

What is pain?

Physical pain is felt by the receptor cells of our nerve endings sending a chemical and electrical code to the brain. The brain reads the code and sends back a response: the alert of pain.

In the presence of pain, all other signals are ignored and pain is given top priority, alerting the entire body to respond. This affects all the body's functions: blood flow, heart rate, digestion, and adrenaline output.

Where are these receptors of pain?

Different parts of the body have a different number of pain receptors. If dust lands on your arm, you may not feel it. But let that same speck of dust fall into your eye, and you are immobilized until it's removed. Your eye is hypersensitive to pain and pressure.

Every part of the body has a unique sensitivity to pain and pressure depending on its function. The face and nose's sensitivity are acute, whereas the foot endures the pressure of the body's weight stomping on it all day.

The fingertips have a special hypersensitivity. Because of their constant use, they are sensitive to pressure and temperature, enabling the blind to "see" with them. Yet with all this sensitivity, they can still handle more impact with less pain than some other parts of the body.

What about the vital organs? Because they are "vital," they have four times more pain receptors cells than other parts of the body.

How do pain receptors work?

When you sit, you never sit still. You fidget. You move. Your brain tells your hip and leg cells to shift weight. They obey.

This communication between the brain and the nerve cells whispers subconsciously, "Ease up. Rest." When the message is ignored, it becomes a shout. Blisters form to change the behavior.

What if these cells don't tell of pain?

Consider a person with leprosy. His nerve cells don't respond to pain stimuli. He feels nothing. He is pain free! But if he walks five miles, he returns with foot ulcers that could result in amputation. Why? He doesn't feel pain.

A healthy person changes the way he walks from the first mile to the fifth mile. Pain cells in his toes, heels, arches, and lateral bones tell the brain to rest and to adjust. All the changes are performed subconsciously. Every spot on a healthy person's body is talking to the brain.

Pain is good. Pain tells us to change our behavior.

When a person twists his ankle, his brain tells his body to remove all weight from his leg immediately. He falls, protecting his ankle from further harm. Later, limping compensates for the damage and redirects the weight and pressure from the injured cells.

Take the same accident with someone who has leprosy. He twists his ankle. There is no pain signal. He continues walking on the foot, even though the bottom of the foot is turned completely inward. He walks without a limp. He has just irreparably damaged his left lateral ligament. He lacked the protection of pain. Due to more complications, his leg may eventually be amputated.

Is pain good?

Paul Brand tells the story of a leprosy patient who was released for a weekend trip home after four years of extensive surgeries and preventative care training. His visit home would prove that he could lead a normal life.

After the first night, he rose to examine himself. To his dismay, he found his finger mangled. By the blood and marks, he knew his finger had been gnawed by a rat. Unable to find a rat trap for the next night, he determined to stay awake to prevent further harm. That night, unable to fight sleep any more, his hand slipped to one side against the hot glass of a hurricane lamp. On the second morning, he found his skin burned off. The man lost both of his hands because he had no signal for pain.

He returned to the doctor who had conducted all his prior surgeries and had trained him to prevent injury. "I feel as if I've lost all my freedom. How can I be free without pain?"[1]

Pain signals something is wrong.
Is pain good? Absolutely.
Can a good God give suffering?
God gave us pain for our protection, for our good.
God is good.

---

[1] Brand and Yancey, p. 239.

DOES GOD CARE ABOUT OUR PAIN?

Pain—whether physical, emotional or spiritual—is good. All pain is a symptom; not the disease. It alerts us to danger. It causes us to change our actions to prevent further harm. Weariness warns us that rest is needed or a breakdown will come. Guilt is uncomfortable in order to bring us to repentance and forgiveness.

Even though we see that pain is for our good—alerting to danger, alarming for change—we still find ourselves asking, "Does God care?"

In Jeremiah 22:16, God commended King Josiah for being like Him in caring for others' pain. *"He pled the cause of the afflicted and needy; then it was well. Is not that what it means to know Me?"*

In Exodus 3:7,8 the Lord saw the affliction of His people and heard their cry. *"...for I am aware of their sufferings. So I have come down to deliver them from the power of the Egyptians."*

God saw His creation in pain and came to their rescue. But He didn't stop there. He took His love another step.

Think about the leper trained to see the warning and change his behavior, yet who still doesn't *feel* pain. Can he understand your pain from your sprained ankle? No.

Having a God Who knows *about* pain is not enough. We crave a God Who is affected by our suffering. By looking to Jesus, we have such a God. *"He existed in the form of God . . . but emptied Himself . . . being made in the likeness of men . . . . He humbled Himself by becoming obedient to . . . death on a cross."* Philippians 2:6-8

Jesus, Who was God, became man. He demonstrated to the

world that He opposed illness and suffering. Never during His earthly life did He decline healing or tell anyone to "be happy with your illness." Instead, He fulfilled Isaiah's prophesy in Luke 4:18. He preached the gospel to the poor, released the captives, gave sight to the blind, and set free the oppressed.

Not only did Jesus spend his ministry eliminating pain in others, He chose to experience suffering and death. His death was not taken from him, as a martyr. His death was a free-will offering: "*not what I will, but what You will*" Mark 14:36.

Jesus's physical suffering on the cross is not what makes the difference in our lives. (Others have died without just cause.) Nor is the cross the worst torture that can be afflicted. (Fox's Book of Martyrs tells of deaths more horrible than crucifixion.)

The cross of Christ makes the difference in our suffering because it shows God suffering. God joined Himself to man by stepping from heaven, confined in a human body in place and time for *His creation* to shame, scourge and abuse.

Isaiah captures the pain of God as the suffering servant in Isaiah 53. Read the entire chapter with God's suffering in mind. These excerpts show a glimpse of what God suffered.

"*He was despised and forsaken* [by the very men He created],
A man of sorrows and acquainted with grief . . . *He was despised, and we did not esteem Him.*
Surely our griefs He himself bore,
And our sorrows He carried;
But He was pierced through for our transgressions,
He was crushed for our iniquities;
The chastening for our well-being fell upon Him, (His love for us found a way to atone for our sins and reconcile us to His holiness.)
And by His scourging we are healed . . . .
But the Lord has caused the iniquity of us all to fall on Him. (Without Him, we would be lost)
He was oppressed and He was afflicted . . . .
But the Lord was pleased [thought it good] *to crush Him, putting Him to grief.*
If He would render Himself as a guilt offering . . . .
As a result of the anguish of His soul,
He will see it and be satisfied . . . .
Because He poured out Himself to death,
And was numbered with the transgressors; (all of us—falling short of His glory)

Yet He himself bore the sin of many,
And interceded for the transgressors." (His love makes a way for us.)

The God-Man Jesus Christ stepped into time, space, and sorrow, limiting Himself to experience our pain, overthrowing the powers of this world by allowing sin to do its worst to Him. An innocent sacrifice was offered.

By His resurrection, He conquered and destroyed anything that would interfere with His love for His creation. *"Neither death, nor life, nor angels, nor principalities, nor things present, nor things to come, nor powers, nor height, nor depth, nor any other created thing, will be able to separate us from the love of God, which is in Christ Jesus our Lord"* Romans 8:38-39.

God uses His own Son's death to give our pain meaning.

Our pain is swallowed up in His death. *"That I may know Him and the power of His resurrection and the fellowship of His sufferings, being conformed to His death; in order that I may attain to the resurrection from the dead"* Philippians 3:10-11.

God enters into our pain. What we endure becomes a part of His suffering and results in triumph and good. Our sorrow is given meaning.

In Matthew 25:35-40, Jesus identified Himself with suffering. *"'For I was hungry, and you gave Me something to eat; I was thirsty, and you gave Me something to drink; I was a stranger, and you invited Me in; naked, and you clothed Me; I was sick, and you visited Me; I was in prison, and you came to Me.'*

"Then the righteous will answer Him, 'Lord, when did we see You hungry, and feed You, or thirsty, and give You something to drink? And when did we see You a stranger, and invite You in, or naked, and clothe You? When did we see You sick, or in prison, and come to You?'

"The King will answer and say to them, 'Truly I say to you, to the extent that you did it to one of these brothers of Mine even the least of them, you did it to Me.'"

Another example of how the Lord feels our suffering. On the road to Damascus, the Lord asks Saul, the persecutor of His people, "Saul, why are you persecuting *Me*?"

After these arguments, it seems inappropriate to ask, "Why does God allow the innocent to suffer?" The question should be, "Why does God allow Himself to suffer?"

The only answer worthy of such a God is, because of His great love for me.

WHY DOES A LOVING GOD MAKE US SUFFER?

Human suffering cannot be reconciled with the existence of a loving God unless we know God. There are two basic misconceptions many people have. One, a self-focused definition of love that trivializes its true meaning. And two, the idea that God's primary purpose in creation was to make mankind the supreme center of the universe.

What does it mean to love?

You instruct your son not to run out on the road, not because you want to hinder his fun as he plays ball, but because you want to prevent a car from hitting him. You discipline him when he doesn't obey, and runs out on the street.

You discipline your son, because you wish more than his immediate happiness, you desire his character to be disciplined. But you do not reprimand your neighbor's son for wrong doing, because you don't care intimately about his character and thus his happiness.

The parallel is true with God and His creation. He disciplines those who are His.

The Creator values what He has created.

By wishing for less suffering, we wish not for more love but for less.

If we look at God as an artist and us the sketch, we wish He would be satisfied with a quick sketch of what He wants of us. Instead, He labors over the painting, blending colors here and making definite marks there.

The Bible speaks of the Church as the Lord's bride. Christ desires no spot or wrinkle. Love forgives all shortcomings, but desires their removal. Christ's goal is to present His bride perfect, whole, unblemished, to *"be a vessel for honor, sanctified useful to the Master, prepared for every good work"* 2 Timothy 2:21.

To demand that divine love be pleased with us, as we remain in our sin, is to ask God to stop being God. His holiness is repelled by stains. Our happiness is not Christ's goal. He desires us to be like Him. He works to conform us to Himself.

We ask for a God Who loves, and we have One. He will not let us continue to do wrong, because His love desires our best. His love compels us to reach that standard.

Man was created for God, not God for man.

Not only do we wish for a trivial love when we question suffering, but we assume man is the center of things. Man is not the center. God doesn't exist for the sake of man. Man was created for God. *"Worthy are You . . . to receive glory and honor and power; for You created all things, and because of Your will they existed, and were created"* Revelation 4:11. We were created for His pleasure.

Our analogy of the father with his son doesn't completely parallel God's relationship with us, because the father may discipline for his own needs, or his own selfish purposes. But God has no needs. He can give love, but doesn't need us to give it to Him. His love is limitless. He gives everything yet requires nothing, unless He "requires" something of His own choosing.

He chooses, although lacking nothing, to need us—not because we are vital to His well-being, but rather because we need to be needed.[2]

For example, look at God's glory. God's glory cannot be diminished by man refusing to worship Him. Can we stop the sun from shining by going into a dark room and closing our eyes? God cannot stop being Who He is.

God desires our ultimate good. He knows it is good for us to love Him. In order to love Him, we must know Him. When we intimately know Him, we will fall to our faces in worship. We will trust His heart no matter what He allows to happen to us. If we don't, we don't really know God.

God gives us what we need, not what we think we want. What

---

[2] Lewis, p. 50.

we want is not too much love, but too little.

We are short-sighted when we ask, "Why does God make us suffer?"

God's love is not what we could imagine. Our thoughts aren't God's thoughts. His plans are for our good, far beyond what we could ever ask or even imagine.

WHY DOES GOD ALLOW US TO CHOOSE A PATH OF PAIN?

When God created the world, He created everything for Himself. God pronounced all creation "good." And man was "very good." God made man in His own image with a will, spirit, and soul to communicate with Him (Genesis 1:26).

With that will came the possibility of a "won't." A will implies a choice. A choice implies consequences. God gave a choice between good and evil. Choosing good, obedience to God, would result in blessing. Choosing evil, disobedience, would result in punishment.

God did not create wrong. But God created man with the ability to choose wrong.

Adam chose to reject God's way and chose his own way. By allowing Adam such a choice, evil came into the world.

Choices have consequences.

"The Lord . . . gives to each man according to his ways, according to the results of his deeds." Jeremiah 17:10.

We chose wrong. Fellowship with God was broken.

"All of us like sheep have gone astray, each of us has turned to his own way" Isaiah 53:6.

"'For My thoughts are not your thoughts, nor are your ways My ways,' declares the Lord" Isaiah 55:8.

By man's choice, he now knows the pain of a broken creation.

To allow choice is to allow for the consequence of pain, but without choice there can't be love.

For us to love, choice is required.

Mandatory love is not love, but fulfilled duty. Love requires a choice: a willful act. If we could love without thought or will, love would merely be an obligation fulfilled. That isn't love.

God gave us the ability to choose, not so we could experience pain, but so we could love Him. God desires a relationship with us.

God wanted us to know Him intimately. He didn't just want an intellectual knowledge of Who He is, but a heart-bonding fellowship. Only love could bring that.

In order to achieve that fellowship, God gave us choice. By choosing Him, we choose love, light, perfection, truth, goodness, and everything else that God is. By not choosing Him, we reject all those things and embrace their opposites.

God made two perfect people, put them in a perfect environment, gave them perfect instructions, yet allowed them to choose whether or not to love Him.

They didn't.

God waits for man to turn back to Him.

But He also knows we can never find our way back to Him without His help.

In His love, God made a way for man to come back into fellowship.

But still, man chooses his own way.

The story Jesus told of the prodigal son shows the father waiting for his wayward son's return. It parallels God's love for us.

Do you have a grown child who has forsaken your instruction?

God did. Here's what He said:

"There is hope for your future,' declares the Lord, 'and your children will return to their own territory. I have surely heard Ephraim grieving, "You have chastised me, and I was chastised, like an untrained calf; bring me back that I may be restored, for You are the Lord my God. For after I turned back, I repented; and after I was instructed, I smote on my thigh; I was ashamed and also humiliated because I bore the reproach of my youth."

"'Is Ephraim My dear son? Is he a delightful child? Indeed, as often as I have spoken against him, I certainly still remember him; therefore My heart yearns for him; I will surely have mercy on him,' declares the Lord" Jeremiah 31:17-20.

Here and in the parable of the prodigal son, the father didn't change his standard and accept his son's riotous life, but he waited for his son's repentance.

The father hurt for the son. His pain was greater than the son's pain. Why? Because he knew the sorrow the son would experience, long before the son felt it.

But love let him go.

He waited for the son's return.

What about the mom who poured all her love into her son?

She gave her life for his happiness.

Still that son rejected the right way, and ignored his spiritual training.

Will she doubt God's holiness? Will she wonder if God's Law is essential? (It's not written in stone, or was it?)

Does the pain now cause her to doubt God's goodness?

Maybe she doubts whether truth is worth it.

She worries whether her son will come back.

Or does she instead look to her Father?

His holiness, goodness, truth, and timing holds her secure, even when she has questions.

Does she consider how God responded to the pain of His creatures' rejection of Him? Did He react in self-pity at how man had wasted His gift of love?

No, the Father stood waiting . . . in love.

In time, the son returned, repentant.

Love lets us choose.

Love holds us accountable for our choices.

Love waits.

But then, love forgives when we repent.

When we return, the father says, "Let's celebrate. Let's tell everyone."

When I have pain caused by a son I bore, have I given it to the One Who can hold the pain?

Only by God's help.

Is it a one-time offering?

Absolutely not.

It's a moment-by-moment gift as I consciously offer that pain as a sacrifice to God.

It's a reminder to me to remind my Father; Who hasn't forgotten, but is waiting as eagerly as I am to see my son return.

But it takes a long time . . . .

God isn't bound by time. He sees yesterday as today and even tomorrow.

The wrong of yesterday brings discipline today, until the final hope of reconciliation tomorrow.

I don't like time.

I want it now.

Maybe I'm too much like my son, who wanted his pleasure now.

I want discipline and restoration now.

But God in His plan holds time in His Hand. (Just like the pain.)

I must rest in His standard of what is good and in the hope He promised for those who seek Him.

In this time of waiting, God works with my son.

But He also works with me.

I see God's holiness by His rules.

I see God's justice by the discipline He metes out to offenders.

I see God's love by the forgiveness He offers to those rebelling against His rules.

I see God's plan through time to conform me to His image, no matter what it takes, or how long.

He wants my fellowship.

How does He get that fellowship?

Through His love.

How does He show His love?

By bringing pain.

Without pain, I forget Him.

So He makes it hurt: for the mom as well as the son.

I lift my son before the throne of his Father.

He hears my petition.

But more than that.

He welcomes my presence.

I learn what it means, not to just know His rules, but to know *Him*.

I find peace in His presence, even in pain.

God gives us choice so we can love Him. But with choice comes the possibility of pain. With the pain, He brings purpose: to draw us back to Himself. And so we see again the love of God wooing us to know Him.

WHY DO BAD THINGS HAPPEN TO GOOD PEOPLE?

Most of us sympathize with the dying man who said, "What harm have I ever done God?" Can we can live apart from God, yet still please Him? We were made to give Him pleasure. The greatest wrong we do is to ignore Him.

We wish, "Why won't God leave me alone?" But would we want such a God?

God compares your state with Himself. And we all fall short.

We compare our goodness to others and find safety. We're just fine, we think, because we're better than someone else. We think God sees us as a group. He doesn't. We stand before Him alone—undone.

"Sowing wild oats" in youth, then settling down after the wild teenage years, gives a false impression that time cancels sin. Time does not absolve our actions. We will stand before Him with our entire life before Him.

The standard of goodness is not fallen man nor enough time erasing our actions.

God compares our state with Himself.

We all fall short.

What was that first sin?
Our first sin was not against our neighbor such as a social sin of unkindness. Nor was it just disobeying God's command. The consequences don't justify the disobedience. Adam and Eve were cast from the Garden. They were separated from God.

Before the fall, man's thoughts centered on God and what pleased Him. Adam and Eve honored and reverenced and adored

Him! They walked and talked with Him. He delighted in them and they in Him.

The first sin was a rejection of the reason God made them—for His pleasure. The fall turned man's thoughts from God to himself. "I will be like God." Self ruled.

Man's very purpose for life—to please God, to delight in Him, to love Him with their total being—was broken. We are undone. We are guilty. *"For My thoughts are not your thoughts, nor are your ways My ways, declares the Lord. For as the heavens are higher than the earth, so ares My ways higher than your ways and My thoughts than your thoughts"* Isaiah 55:8,9.

"We are not merely imperfect creatures needing to be improved but rebels who must lay down our arms."[3]

We were created to know and enjoy God and be complete in Him. But by our sin, we can't fulfill our designed purpose. Our true pleasure is gone.

How do we return to that self-surrendered life that gives us happiness?

Nothing but redemption through His Son's blood can complete the work of rejuvenation in our hearts and minds to make us pleasing in His sight.

To render back to God our self-will is a painful kind of death. When disciplining a child, the first step is to make the child give up his self-will. He must will to do what his father's desires. We, too, must die daily to self.

Why? Because our Father knows that unless we die to our flesh, we cannot live by His Spirit.

Dying to ourselves is hard. We fight against dying, because we can't see the big picture that our Father sees. So God, in love, brings pain to redirect our desires. Just as a loving father punishes a child who plays ball out on the road. The child doesn't consider how a passing car can kill him. He just wants to play ball. He thinks he knows better than his dad. He does wrong until pain redirects his desire.

Before pain, we deceive ourselves that all is well. We don't need God. We have all we want. God is an interruption.

Pain forces us to see that all is not well.

---

3 Lewis, p. 91.

God is *not* pleased. God interrupts to show us, we need Him.

Because God made us, He knows our happiness lies in Him. We don't seek Him. Our self-sufficiency makes surrender repulsive. God must show us how dangerous our self-sufficiency is.

This self-sufficiency may be the strongest in kind, honest, "good" people. They don't see their need for God, if they can do "good" things themselves. But God causes them to see nothing but Him. He removes the false happiness of self-sufficiency and draws all men to Himself.

St. Augustine said, "God is always trying to give good things us, but our hands are too full to receive them."

Good people with their good lives don't look to God.

God, in His love, strips away anything that comes between us and dependence upon Him. We have no other option. We must look up. We find Him sufficient.

The problem is not why some kind, good people suffer, but why some do not.

We see that God blesses us more than we deserve. We again find God's love is more than we can imagine.

We need Him. His sufficiency is enough. God is pleased.

WHAT SHOULD WE DO WHEN WE SUFFER?

We are made to please Him. But our thoughts are not God's. We only look to God when we can look nowhere else. These things we have learned.

But what about the pain in our world? How does what we've learned help when every day has pain?

Accidents are not as devastating as chronic pain. It's not the mountain that defeats our climb, but the sand in our shoe. All the little things added together weigh our thinking down and break our hearts.

This is true if we are personally experiencing pain, but it's also true when we are involved with others in pain. How do we guard our hearts while we work with those in extreme suffering to prevent burn-out, hypersensitivity and fatigue? For example, working with child abuse victims, one can easily become hypersensitive—seeing abuse where there is none. This quickly leads to skepticism and withdrawal.

Dr. Brand, while working with lepers, wisely cautioned his apprentices not to be totally sensitive to *all* the needs of *all* the patients or they would soon become *insensitive* to all. He asked God to identify one or two select patients with special needs for him to focus on. In this way, he was able to be sensitive without becoming hardened by the endless suffering.

"For you always have the poor with you" Mark 14:7. Poverty won't be eliminated. Pain remains.

We act as the nerve receptor cells. (Remember from the chapter *Can A Good God Give Suffering?)* We receive the message. We relay the message to the Holy Spirit (through prayer), and He transmits the message to Christ, the Head. He receives from His body (His people) the messages of pain that we endure. He feels it. He knows it. He suffers. He returns a message to His body, giving direction about how we should respond to the pain.

Romans 8:26-27 takes on new meaning. *"In the same way the Spirit also helps our weakness; for we do not know how to pray as we should, but the Spirit Himself intercedes for us with groanings too deep for words; and He who searches the hearts knows what the mind of the Spirit is, because He intercedes for the saints according to the will of God."*

We tell God of another's pain, asking for His help. He tells us what to do.

We will not eliminate pain. Nor should we want to, if pain makes us look to God. Sometimes eliminating another's pain is the worst thing we can do for them. There is danger in helping another in pain, if God is seeking their attention. If we interfere, that person may harden his heart away from God, rather than looking to Him for answers. We need to seek God, not only in our own pain, but when we help another.

Look at the prodigal son in Luke 15. Do you think the father didn't know the son's intentions? Do you wonder at the father's willingness to give the irresponsible son all his inheritance? Do you think the father's pain was any less than the son's? (The father hurt long before the son realized he should be hurting.)

John Wesley's mother was once asked, "Which one of your eleven children do you love the most?" Her wise answer reflects the anguish of a parent's heart: "I love the one who's sick until he's well, the one who's away until he comes home." *A parent is only as happy as his most hurting child.*

Does that mean we keep them home and choose for them so that they don't choose poorly? We let go, watch the Heavenly Father's face, learn His thoughts and find peace in Him.

"Consider it all joy, my brethren, when you encounter various trials, knowing that the testing of your faith produces endurance. And let endurance have its perfect result, so that you may be perfect and complete, lacking in nothing. But if any of you lacks wisdom, let him ask of God, who gives to all generously and without reproach, and it will be given to him. But he must ask in faith without any doubting, for the one who doubts is like the surf of the sea, driven and tossed by the wind" James 1: 2-6.

We may be quick to say, "I don't understand."

And so we don't. God is God, and we are not. But many times our statement of misunderstanding lies not in the fact that we don't understand, but in our desire to change God, to conform Him to our thinking. That kind of "understanding" will not come.

Acknowledge God is God.
Know that God is good.

Recognize God works all things for His good, even using the wicked for His glory. *The Lord has made everything for its own purpose, even the wicked for the day of evil"* Proverbs 16:4.

These ares the two premises that we started with: God is good and God is in control.

Romans 8:12-25 walks us through the process—from acknowledging our own thoughts lead to death to dying to self helps us to see Him. It's a long passage—do not skip it because it seems familiar to you. Read it with what you now know of suffering.

"So then, brethren, we are under obligation, not to the flesh, to live according to the flesh—for if you are living according to the flesh, you must die; but if by the Spirit you are putting to death the deeds of the body, you will live. For all who are being led by the Spirit of God, these are sons of God. For you have not received a spirit of slavery leading to fear again, but you have received a spirit of adoption as sons by which we cry out, 'Abba! Father!'

"The Spirit Himself testifies with our spirit that we are children of God. And if children, heirs also, heirs of God and fellow heirs with Christ, if indeed we suffer with Him so that we may also be glorified with Him.

"For I consider that the sufferings of this present time are not worthy to be compared with the glory that is to be revealed to us. For the anxious longing of the creation waits eagerly for the revealing of the sons of God. For the creation was subjected to futility, not willingly, but because of Him who subjected it, in hope that the creation itself also will be set free from its slavery to corruption into the freedom of the glory of the children of God.

"For we know that the whole creation groans and suffers the pains of childbirth together until now. And not only this, but also we ourselves, having the first fruits of the Spirit, even we ourselves groan within ourselves, waiting eagerly for our adoption as sons, the redemption of our body. For in hope we have been saved, but hope that is seen is not hope; for who hopes for what he already sees? But if we hope for what we do not see, with perseverance we wait eagerly for it."

Do you see God wooing us by suffering to bring our wayward thoughts to Him? Right after this passage is Romans 8:26-27—the passage we looked at about the Spirit petitioning for our requests as we bare our hearts before Him. Can you feel the heartbeat of the Father? Do you know He cares for you?

Do you want to hear the final words that God gives after the suffering, after directing your thoughts to Him, after recognizing your self-sufficiency is not enough?

"And we know that God causes all things to work together for good to those who love God, to those who are called according to His purpose. For those whom He foreknew, He also predestined to become conformed to the image of His Son, so that He would be the firstborn among any brethren; and these whom He predestined, He also called; and these whom He called, He also justified; and these whom He justified, He also glorified" Romans 8:28-30.

What does God say after we have been stripped of our own self-sufficiency and been conformed to His likeness?

It is good.

Does He leave us stripped, exposed and needy? Look at the final verses of that chapter, Romans 8:31-39.

"What then shall we say to these things? If God is for us, who is against us? He who did not spare His own Son, but delivered Him over for us all, how will He not also with Him freely give us all things? Who will bring a charge against God's elect? God is the one who justifies; who is the one who condemns? Christ Jesus is He who died, yes, rather who was raised, who is at the right hand of God, who also intercedes for us. Who will separate us from the love of Christ? Will tribulation, or distress, or persecution, or famine, or nakedness, or peril, or sword? Just as it is written, 'For Your sake we are being put to death all day long; we were considered as sheep to be slaughtered.' But in all these things we overwhelmingly conquer through Him who loved us. For I am convinced that neither death, nor life, nor angels, nor principalities, nor things present, nor things to come, nor powers, nor height, nor depth, nor any other created thing, will be able to separate us from the love of God, which is in Christ Jesus our Lord."

We are reminded of His love.

Suffering at the hand of a good God (Who suffers more than we do) makes us look to Him, acknowledges our self-sufficiency, and seek to know His thoughts. We have come full circle—for we again see the love of God.

What should we do when we suffer? Acknowledge God's goodness, God's love, God's plan . . . and worship Him.

WHEN I AM HURT BY OTHERS WHAT DO I DO?

The immediate response when people hurt us is to be defensive, make excuses, and execute judgment. We want ourselves preserved. Yet Christ's words ring in our hearts: "Turn the other cheek," and "forgive." How?

What forgiveness is not.

Forgiving is not the same as forgetting.

Just because we forgive someone does not mean the pain they caused will instantly disappear.

Forgiving is not the same as trusting.

When someone with responsibility fails, we forgive his failure, but we may not allow him to have the same position. A position is earned. *"Now it is required that those who have been given a trust must prove faithful"* I Corinthians 4:2.

For example, a husband who has been found unfaithful can be forgiven but must earn back his wife's trust before she can believe him again.

Forgiveness is not an excuse for others to do wrong.

"What shall we say, then? Are we to continue in sin so that grace may increase? May it never be! How shall we who died to sin still live in it?" Romans 6:1-2.

"Bear with each other and forgive whatever grievances you may have against one another. Forgive as the Lord forgave you"

Colossians 3:13.

If repentance isn't sought, should forgiveness be given?
Should you forgive a person who doesn't repent and turn from his wrong?

The Lord forgave while we were still sinning. We weren't seeking His forgiveness. But that is not an excuse to continue to sin.

Peter came to Jesus and asked, *"'Lord, how many times shall I forgive my brother when he sins against me? Up to seven times?'*

"Jesus answered, 'I tell you, not seven times, but seventy-seven times'" Matthew 18:21-22.

Some people don't repent. And some of those people Jesus calls your "brother." That's why it hurts. It's hard. It's personal.

Jesus didn't say they are asking for repentance. He says when your brother sins against you. You forgive when he doesn't ask, because you must—again and again and again.

But as long as they don't repent, or change, restoration can't happen. Trust, fellowship, and communion aren't restored, because unrepented sin separates.

Some say you shouldn't offer forgiveness until the persons asks. but God says "forgive."

When someone hurts me (don't we all have someone like this?), I approach him. If he doesn't acknowledge his wrong, I struggle to forgive. But by God's help, I can let go of the hurt and forgive him. I don't expect him to change. I accept him for who he is, sinner and all. I accept the pain he has caused me. I move forward, something I can't do until I forgive him. His actions won't hold me in bondage

Years later, when he asks forgiveness, I can extend love because I've already forgiven him.. Now, by his admitting his wrong, fellowship can be restored. But because it has been years of brokenness, fellowship will take time. I still won't automatically trust. That must be earned.

How do we forgive?

Forgiveness comes when we give our hurts to God and acknowledge God as judge.
Sometimes we are hurt by people who didn't intend to hurt us. When we confront them and ask them of their intentions, we

find it was a miscommunication. Many grudges and pains aren't intended. Our limited view alters what was meant. When things are discussed, we find the meaning clear and the hurt unintended, a misunderstanding explained. So first, talk to those who have hurt you.

Then for those hurts that are intentional and volitional, forgiveness is made possible when you realize in this world you will be persecuted for doing what is right. You are a light to a dark world. Wrong doesn't like exposure. If someone living in sin can extinguish your light, they feel it makes them look better.

"Bless those who persecute you; bless and do not curse . . . . Never pay back evil for evil to anyone. Respect what is right in the sight of all men. If possible, so far as it depends on you, live at peace with all men. Never take your revenge, beloved, but leave room for the wrath of God, for it is written. 'Vengeance is mine. I will repay, says the Lord.' But if your enemy is hungry, feed him, and if he is thirsty, give him a drink; for in so doing you will heap burning coals on his head. Do not be overcome by evil, but overcome evil with good" Romans 12:14, 17-21.

How do you do that?

My heart wants to hold onto the hurt. My mind wants to recite the injustice. My reaction is to give back what they deserve.

Forgiveness lies in committing to know His thoughts.

"Let your gentle spirit be known to all men. The Lord is near. Be anxious for nothing, but in everything [including your hurts], by prayer and supplication with thanksgiving let your requests be made known to God. And the peace of God, which surpasses all comprehension, will guard your hearts and your minds in Christ Jesus. [Memories of hurts will grow dim.] Finally, brethren, whatever is true [no excuses for our own behavior], . . . honorable . . . right . . . pure . . . lovely . . . if there is any excellence and if anything worthy of praise, dwell on these things. . . . Practice these things. And the God of peace will be with you" Philippians 4:5-9.

When I choose to dwell on God's thoughts (His list is pretty long, but doesn't include what wrongs are done to me), I find *"the peace of God, which passes all comprehension."* That peace *"will guard [our] hearts and [our] minds in Christ Jesus"* Philippians 4:7.

I'd rather have peace than carry a grudge, wouldn't you?

Then seek to know Him.

HOW DO I
RESPOND TO EVIL?

There is a difference between forgiving wrongs and fighting evil.

Government was instituted by God as a means to execute justice and judgment on wrongdoers. It isn't the individual's responsibility to punish wrongdoing. So how are we to respond to evil in this world? The Bible gives three responses: flee, confront and fight.

Flee

When Potiphar's wife pursued him daily, Joseph ran from her presence (Genesis 39:6-18). We don't sit in front of the cookie jar when we're trying to lose weight and hope we can overcome the temptation. We run. The same is true of evil and temptations.

Lot was told to flee Sodom and Gomorrah. He wasn't to stay and fight. The evil had become a part of him and he lost his married daughters and their families. While leaving, he lost his wife because she looked back and became salt. She disobeyed the angel's command. *"Escape for your life! Do not look behind you, and do not stay anywhere in the valley; escape to the mountains, or you will be swept away!"* Genesis 19:17.

Paul warns Timothy of false teachers *"holding to a form of godliness, although they had denied its power: Avoid such men as these."* The false teachers seek those who are *"always learning and never able to come to the knowledge of the truth"* II Timothy 3:5,7.

Years ago, my husband met someone who had questions. Every day this person had more questions. My husband spent weeks answering them. As the days wore into months, and the list of questions continued, our family felt the strain; not just from time away from dad, but also from questions that reflected no desire to learn.

The man was *"always learning and never able to come ot the knowledge of the truth."* He sought to argue the Word, not know it. He wanted to defend his position, not find God's.

Eventually, my husband stopped answering his questions. We felt a burden lifted, oppression relieved. That person was one that we should *"avoid."*

Confront

There are times to compromise, to make peace, to get along—but never with evil. Evil does not compromise. Evil always seeks to control, to conquer, and to consume.

Christ did not forgive evil. He confronted it.

Look at the money changers in the temple (Luke 19:45-48). He didn't flee the evil; he confronted the wrong, and cleaned His Father's house.

When Peter rebuked Christ for teaching them that He would be killed and rise again, Christ rebuked Peter. *"'Get behind me, Satan. . . . You are not setting your mind on God's interests, but man's"* Mark 8:34.

Fight

God doesn't remove you from the world when you become a Christian. He expects you to be a light for Him in the world.

Christ's prayer was *"I do not ask You [the Father] to take them [the believers] out of the world, but to keep them from the evil one. They are not of the world, even as I am not of the world"* John 17:15-16.

We don't isolate ourselves, thinking we'll be able to keep from seeing and experiencing evil. Even if we lived in a nice little commune where we controlled our surroundings, and had special rules that kept us "good," we would still have evil. Why? Because we are evil! Isn't that what Paul talked about in Romans 7:4-25? He fights with his evil desires to do what his spirit knows he should do.

We don't teach our children to keep them *from* the world. We instruct them in the Word, so that they will be ready *for* the world.

If Christians don't confront and fight evil, who will? Evil won't just go away. It commands, controls, and consumes.

So how do we fight it? Ephesians 6:10-17 shows us the armor

that God provides for His children. Truth, righteousness, gospel of peace, faith, salvation, the Word of God, and praying in the Spirit.

When you attack with truth, you stand on something that does not give way.

When you've put on the breastplate of righteousness, you know your vital organs are protected, enabling you to extend your reach to conquer wrong.

When you walk, you spread the gospel to dispel the darkness of sin.

When deceptive ideas come your way, your faith recognizes them and destroys them.

When you become a child of God, you are given the helmet of salvation, protecting you from head injuries; you know Who has redeemed you and given you eternal life.

Your defense for this fight?

Know the Word of God.

You will be exposed to evil. *"Do not be overcome by evil, but overcome evil with good"* Romans 12:21.

A light shining in darkness will cause conflict. Determine whether you must flee, confront or fight. How do you know? By seeking the Spirit through His Word and constant prayer.

His Word gives the victory over evil. Evil may often seem like it's winning, but God will have the final word. *"Until heaven and earth pass away, not the smallest letter or stroke shall pass from the Law until all is accomplished"* Matthew 5:18.

Know Him. Know His Word. The fight will be in His hands as well as will the victory.

HELD BY HIS HANDS

Our Father created the world. He held it in His hands and announced, "It is good."

But we took what His hands made and stained it. Our hands made dirty what His hands had made good.

He sent His Son with hands of an infant to show the world He understood humanity's helplessness and to fix what our hands had done. As Jesus grew, His carpenter hands fashioned wood and stone into gifts for us, a reminder of what He and His Father had created before the world began. His hands, calloused and rough, extended in service. We insulted His gifts and mocked His goodness.

When His ministry began, His physician's hands touched the unclean, the outcasts bringing healing, giving a balm for those seeking peace.

Instead of gratitude, we raised our hands in jealous rage to silence His message and scorn His deliverance.

We drove spikes, paralyzing His Hands into claw shapes unable to feel movement. Even in His death, His hands were outstretched in love to His creation. But death couldn't silence the work of His Hands. Jesus extended His Hands to Thomas, proof of Who He was. Thomas saw those scars and believed, saying, "My Lord and my God."

Why did Jesus keep His scars?

His resurrected body could have been perfect, without flaw. Instead, He carried the reminder of His visit to His creatures— His scars, a lasting image of wounded humanity.

"The pain of man has become the pain of God."[4]

---

4 Brand and Yancey, pp. 289-291.

BIBLIOGRAPHY

Brand, Paul and Philip Yancey. *In His Image.* Grand Rapids, MI: Zondervan Publishing House, 1987

Lewis, C.S. *The Problem of Pain.* NY: Macmillan Publishing Co., Inc., 1962.

PLEASE HIM

We are created to please God. But because of our self-ruling nature, we can't.

God sent His Son to bring us back to Himself. By His Son's death, as our substitute, our sin was paid.

When we repent and trust in His Son, we please Him.

But we can't please Him on our own. We must die daily to our self-rule through His Spirit's help in order to please the Father.

Suffering has worked its purpose. We are saved by His sufferings. We are reminded to stay close to Him by our sufferings. We learn what it means to please Him.

ABOUT THE AUTHOR

Sonya Contreras can't claim any suffering in her life, unless one counts struggling through science degrees at Cedarville University or Institute for Creation Research. Marrying her best friend certainly didn't bring any suffering, only a better understanding of God's love. But suffering seemed close when she disciplined her eight sons. She shares her struggles over her own self-ruling nature when she *writes about what matters* at www.sonyacontreras.com.

OTHER BOOKS BY SONYA CONTRERAS

Tell of My Kingdom's Glory Series tells the love story between God and His people.

In **Book One:** ***Until My Name Is Known,*** God brings His people to see Him as He frees them from the bonds of Egypt.

In **Book Two:** ***I Have Called You by Name,*** God draws His people to know Him, as He provides safety through the demands of His Law and teaches dependence upon Him to reach their Land.

In **Book Three:** ***I Am with You,*** God reassures His people that, as He had been with Moses, so would He be with them. He brings them into the Land promised them, giving rest from their journey.

Our Story of His Lessons: Twenty Years of Christmas News

People ask about our boys and how we do it. The yearly letters found here give you a glimpse into those answers.

We've lived in the foothills of the Sequoias for over eighteen years. Almost half of the boys were born in the house. We've set down roots, not only in our garden and with our animals but in our hearts where the land has helped us settle. We share memories on a yearly basis of what God teaches us, thus the chronicles of the Christmas letters.

Let Her Hear: Parables from a Mom

These parables (devotionals) are not a substitute for careful, study of the Word. They give a starting point to focus on where God wants you to be all day, a help to see

Him even while doing the mundane, routine, necessary, "mom" things in life. They remind you of the heavenly realm that's part of the earthly walk.

They were taken from articles previously written for my website and made into book form.

How Suffering Shows God's Love: A Paradox Explained

Pain opens the heart to search for meaning. We ask God, "Why?" and find He is silent. We question His goodness, love, and sovereignty. These questions bring us to Him.

By coming to Him, we learn the deeper answers. We find the love we crave. We discover the God Who wants us to know Him.

This collection of articles leads us to find that meaning, learn those answers, and see our God.

Expecting Jesus

See Jesus through the eyes of those who met Him. Most expected Him. Only a few were ready for Him. These vignettes show what they expected from Jesus. Simeon looked for the hope of Israel. He found Him. Salazar watched for the Coming One and was shown His star in the East. James struggled to believe, until he put aside his assumptions. Others came with theirs expectations.

Put your own expectations aside. Know Him by the truth He reveals to you.

A current listing of books with summaries and excerpts can be found at www.sonyacontreras.com